Birds

Written by Malcolm Penny
Illustrated by Michael Posen

p

This is a Parragon Publishing Book
First published in 2000

Parragon
Queen Street House
4 Queen Street
Bath BA1 1HE, UK

ISBN 0-75254-315-6

Printed in Singapore

Produced by
Monkey Puzzle Media Ltd
Gissing's Farm
Fressingfield
Suffolk IP21 5SH
UK

Designer: Sarah Crouch
Cover design: Victoria Webb
Editor: Linda Sonntag
Artwork commissioning:
Roger Goddard-Coote
Project manager: Alex Edmonds

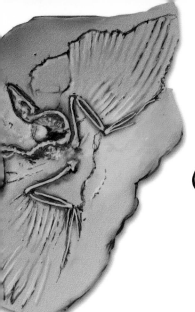

Contents

Do birds have fingers?

YES, THREE OF THEM. THE FIRST, THE THUMB, SUPPORTS A SMALL BUT important part of the wing called the alula, or bastard wing; the second and third support the main flight feathers.

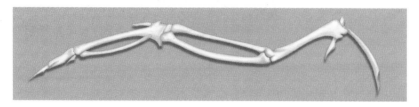

The skeleton of a bird's wing

Why do birds' knees bend backwards?
They don't. What looks like the bird's knee is in fact its ankle, and below it is an extended foot bone, leading to the toes. Its real knee is usually hidden by feathers.

Which bird has the longest wings?
The wandering albatross has a wingspan – the distance from one wingtip to the other, when the wings are stretched out – of more than 9 feet. The longest ever measured was a male with a wingspan of 5 feet (3.45 m); females are usually smaller.

Which birds trot on lillies?
Jacanas are sometimes called "lily-trotters": they live on ponds and lakes, walking on lily pads, to catch the insects that live on them. Their long toes spread their weight out, so that the leaves don't bend and sink.

Jacana

How many toes do birds have?
Two, three or four. A typical perching bird has three pointing forward, and one back; birds that run on hard ground have only three, all pointing forward. Ostriches have only two toes, shaped rather like the hoof of an antelope. Woodpeckers have two toes pointing forward and two back; owls can turn their fourth toe either forward or backward, for perching on a branch, or to get a better grip on prey. Swifts have all four toes pointing forwards.

Why don't birds fall off a branch when they go to sleep?
Tendons, from the tips of the toes, pass behind the ankle joint. This joint is bent when the bird sits down, so the toes are automatically clenched round the twig it is standing on. No muscle power is involved in this grip, so the bird can sleep, without danger of falling.

What is a wishbone?
Sometimes called the "merrythought," the wishbone is created by the bird's collarbones being joined together at their inner ends. This forms a curved strut holding the wings apart while the bird is flying. The strongest fliers have the widest angles in their wishbones.

A jacana walking on lily pads.

Bald eagle

The sharp, hooked beak of an American bald eagle helps it tear apart its prey.

Why do some birds have hooked beaks?

FOR CATCHING AND TEARING THEIR PREY. HAWKS, EAGLES, AND VULTURES, but also owls and shrikes, need to be able to take a firm grip on struggling prey animals, and then pull them apart to eat them. The edges of an eagle's beak act like a pair of scissors, to cut through skin and flesh. Gulls have a sharp hook at the tip of their bill to hold on to slippery fish or squid.

Can a bird change the shape of its beak?

Yes! An oystercatcher's beak changes in a few weeks, from short and blunt while it is eating cockles and mussels, to long and narrow when its diet changes to worms and other soft prey.

Why are bird bones filled with air?

The long bones of birds are like tubes, often with criss-crossing inside, to make them stronger for their weight. Not all birds have equally hollow bones: those that dive into water, like gannets, terns, and kingfishers, and those that fly very fast, like swifts and some waders, have less air in their long bones.

What keeps a bird up in the air?

The shape of its wings. The upper surface is raised in a curve, so that air traveling above it has to move faster, than air moving under the wing. Air moving faster is at a lower pressure than slower air, so the higher pressure under the wing pushes it upwards, as it moves through the air. The first humans to discover how this "aerofoil section" works were Australian Aborigines, when they invented the boomerang.

What is the world's fastest bird?

People will always argue about this. Most think that the peregrine falcon is the fastest bird by far, but when its speed was accurately measured, the maximum in level flight was 58 mph (96 kph). Measurements by radar show that eider ducks fly for long periods at 45 mph (75 kph), but the world record is held by the Asian spine-tailed swift, which has been timed at 102 mph (170 kph) in level flight.

Why do geese fly in a V?

When a bird is flying, the air just behind its wingtips swirls upwards. If another bird flies in this turbulent, rising air, it can save about 15% of the energy it would have to use, if it were flying alone. In a V-formation, the leader is the only bird not saving energy: other birds take its place from time to time, to share the burden of leadership. Swans and cranes are among other birds that use this technique.

What has wing shape to do with flight?

Birds' wings are shaped differently depending on how they need to fly. Fast flight demands narrow wings, like those of swallows, while quick flight in woodland needs short, rounded wings, like those of a bluetit. Falcons change the shape of their wings from long and narrow for fast flight, to swept-back for diving at top speed. Gannets have long wings for long-distance flight and gliding: when they dive to catch fish they fold their stretched wings backwards, like the flights of a dart.

What bird can fly for six hours without moving its wings?

WITH ITS LONG, NARROW WINGS, AN ALBATROSS IS PERFECTLY adapted for gliding, even in still air. But when it glides close to the sea surface, it can make use of wind currents from the waves, giving it an almost continuous source of lift, meaning that in this type of flight, it only has to hold its wings still.

Black browed albatross

The albatross can soar for as long as six hours without moving its wings.

Which chick flies on its birthday?

The chicks of the mallee fowl in Australia, which emerge from the heap of warm sand where they hatched, immediately fly up to a branch to roost in safety. They have to look after themselves from the first day: their parents do not look after them at all.

What is the heaviest bird in the air?

The Kori bustard, from East and South Africa, weighs about 31 lb (14 kg): the largest specimen known weighed just over 40 lb (18 kg). Because it finds flying such hard work, the Kori bustard flies only in emergencies, and only for short distances.

How do birds land?

Ideally, by stalling (ceasing to move forward) just as they touch down. Large water birds, like swans, can water-ski to a halt on outstretched feet. Boobies and albatrosses, which spend most of the year at sea, often crash and tumble over when they finally return to land to breed.

Bee hummingbird

The bee hummingbird hovers as it feeds from a flower.

How does a hummingbird hover?

BY KEEPING ITS BODY NEARLY VERTICAL WHILE ITS WINGS BEAT FORWARD AND backward. It is actually flying upward just fast enough to balance its body weight, so that it stays still. A ruby-throated hummingbird, which weighs less than 0.2 oz, has to beat its wings more than 52 times a second to hover in front of a flower.

What is the slowest bird in the world?

Surprisingly, swifts are also among the slowest-flying birds, moving at less than 12 mph (20 kph) while they are feeding. Their insect prey moves only slowly, so they must move slowly to gather it. They fly faster than this at other times, as they wheel and swoop close to buildings and people. Another answer to this question could be hummingbirds, because when they hover they move at 0 mph! Even better, they are the only birds that can fly backward under power, registering a negative speed!

Which is the smallest migrant bird?

The rufous hummingbird, less than 4 in (9 cm) long, flies every year from Alaska to its winter quarters in Mexico, a round trip of 3,800 miles (6,400 km).

Why are lighthouses dangerous?

The beams from lighthouses attract migrating birds, especially during misty conditions. Many birds are killed when they fly into the glass.

Why do migrating birds fly so far?

TO MOVE OUT OF AREAS, WHICH ARE SUITABLE FOR BREEDING , back to places where they can survive the winter. The reason for moving back to the breeding area is usually because it contains plenty of food in the summer to feed the chicks.

Why do some birds stay behind?

In Sweden, female and young chaffinches migrate south in winter, but some males stay behind in their breeding territories. European blackbirds do the same: it seems that the males, that stay behind through the winter, can hold on to the best breeding territories, for when the females return in spring.

How do birds sense cold weather coming?

Some ducks and geese migrate when the weather finally turns cold enough, but most birds leave long before the winter comes: marsh warblers start to migrate in July. Their bodies tell them when to go, as changes in hormones cause them to put on fat ready for the journey. The final trigger to move is the length of the day, which gets shorter in the fall and longer in spring.

When do birds behave like sailors?

When birds migrate, they use a mixture of signs, including the position of the Sun and stars for navigating on long-distance flights. They also use local landmarks when they are near their destination. They have a "compass" in their heads with which they can sense the earth's magnetic field, and choose their direction accordingly.

How did a bored nobleman discover migration?

The best evidence that birds migrate comes from banding – attaching light, numbered metal bands to birds' legs and releasing the birds in the hope that they will be found again. The first banding experiment was during the French Revolution of 1789, when a nobleman fixed a copper ring to the leg of a swallow, and noticed that it came back to the same nest for three years in a row.

Where did people think swallows went in winter?

They thought that they hibernated, perhaps in hollow trees, or even in the mud at the bottom of ponds. This is not as crazy as it sounds: in cold weather swallows often roost in groups in hollow trees or chimneys, and in spring they can be seen collecting mud at the edge of pools to make their nests.

Which bird spends its whole life in the summer?

The arctic tern breeds in the Arctic, to within 430 miles (720 km) of the North Pole, and migrates every year to the Antarctic, a total distance of 23,000 miles (38,400 km) between breeding seasons. It spends its whole life in the summer.

Pigeons

Pigeons are strong-flying birds and good navigators.

How fast do migrating birds fly?

STUDIES USING RADAR SHOW THAT SMALL BIRDS LIKE WARBLERS MOVE AT ABOUT 21 mph (35 kph) when they are migrating, and ducks at about 42 mph (70 kph). They usually fly for only about six or eight hours a day, but one knot ringed in England was found in Liberia, 3,400 miles (5,600 km) away, only eight days later. It had covered an average distance of 420 miles (700 km) per day; since knots fly at about the same speed as ducks, it must have been traveling for 10 hours every day.

Quetzal

Which birds dig holes to nest in?

MANY BIRDS DIG HOLES FOR their nests, including kingfishers and sand martins, in sandy banks, and woodpeckers in trees. Puffins clean out disused rabbit burrows, the quetzal, in Central America, scoops out a large hole in a rotting tree trunk.

Which birds make the biggest nests?
Eagles. A bald eagle nest in Ohio, USA, which was used for 35 years, was more than 8 feet (2.5 m) across and 12 feet (3.6 m) deep, weighing 1.8 tons. Another in Florida was even bigger: nearly 10 feet (3 m) wide and more than 20 feet (6 m) deep.

Which birds can tie knots?
Many of the African weaver finches start their spherical hanging nests by tying blades of grass to a twig with neat, strong knots.

How do birds learn to build nests?
They know instinctively what to do and what materials to use, but older birds build better nests than beginners. This suggests that they get better with practice, and also that they know where to find the best materials.

Which birds treat their nests with pesticide?
European starlings do. Before the female begins nesting in a hole in a tree, the male bird gathers pieces of green vegetation and puts them into the hole. Scientists have discovered that the male chooses plants that give off certain chemicals which kill parasites, such as bird lice. This helps to keep the nest – and the baby birds that are born in it – free from lice.

The ancient Aztecs and Mayas worshipped the quetzal bird as the god of the air.

Which bird lays the world's smallest egg?

THE SMALLEST IS THAT OF THE BEE HUMMINGBIRD, WHICH IS

just under 0.5 in by 0.25 in (11 by 8 mm), and weighs 0.02 oz (barely anything at all). The egg of the emperor penguin weighs just over one per cent of the weight of the female.

Hummingbird egg

Ostrich egg

From the smallest to the largest – compare the size of an ostrich egg with a hummingbird egg!

What birds lay their eggs in a compost heap?

Mound birds, in Australia and New Guinea dig large holes in the sandy ground, and lay their eggs on a pile of rotting vegetation they have collected in the bottom. The compost warms the eggs from below, and the sun warms them from above. The parents remove or add sand to keep the temperature constant. After all this work, when the chicks hatch the parents aren't at all interested!

What is bird's nest soup?

A Far Eastern delicacy, a soup or jelly made from the sticky cement that cave swiftlets use to stick twigs and feathers together to make their nests. Some species use only their saliva for this, produced from glands in their mouth: their cement is said to be the best for making soup.

Which bird lays a wopper?

The biggest egg is laid by the ostrich: it measures 7 by 5 inches (170 by 135 mm) and weighs 3 lb (1400 g). The biggest egg for the size of the mother is laid by the kiwi, whose eggs, 5 inches (12.5 cm) long, can weigh as much as 1 lb (500 g), a third of the weight of the bird.

Which birds live in communities?

Some, like the sociable weavers of Africa, build huge nests occupied by as many as 100 pairs, but more interesting are those that share the nests of different species. The hamerkop in East Africa builds an enormous nest, more than 3 feet across (1 metre) , part of which is shared by gray kestrels and barn owls, sometimes without driving out the original builder.

When does a nest have a roof?

Many small birds, especially in the tropics, build domed nests, with a roof to protect them from rain and sun. The roof might be made of almost anything, from strands of grass, in weaver nests, to bits of plant tied together with spider's webs, in the nests of sunbirds. In Europe, swallows and long-tailed or penduline tits are the best-known domed nest builders.

What's so good about being sat upon?

Most birds keep their eggs warm by sitting on them – so that the embryo can develop – until they hatch. After hatching, the chicks need to be protected from heat as well as cold: many birds shade their chicks in sunny weather.

This lesser whitethroat is feeding a cuckoo chick that hatched in its nest.

Why is it a good idea to hatch first?

A partridge might take three weeks to lay 15 eggs, only incubating them when the last is laid, so that they all hatch together. Owls, eagles, herons and gulls on the other hand, incubate their eggs as soon as the first one is laid, so that the chicks hatch at different times. If food is short, the last chicks to hatch will die.

When are baby birds bigger than their parents?

Shearwater chicks have to be able to survive while their parents fly far out to sea to find food, sometimes for as long as 10 days. They can store fat after a meal to keep them going until the next meal. At the peak of their growth, after about 80 days, they can weigh 12 oz (300 g), twice as much as their parents. They are not fed for their last 10 days on the nest, so that they lose enough weight to be able to fly.

Do chicks eat the same as their parents?

OME DO, LIKE CHICKS OF SEABIRDS, WHICH EAT FISH. BUT CHICKS of seed-eating birds usually start life eating insects, because they need the special fats and protein that seeds can't provide. Cuckoo chicks eat whatever their foster-brothers and sisters eat, only much more of it.

Which chicks can't wait to leave home?

Lapwings are a good example of

nidifugous (nest-leaving) chicks: they leave the nest as soon as they can all walk, within hours of hatching. Nidicolous (nest-living) chicks stay much longer, in the case of macaws (large parrots) for as long as three months.

Scarlet macaw

How does a hungry chick get fed first?

A parent feeds the chick that is asking loudest for food. This usually turns out fairly, because chicks that were fed last time the parent came to the nest are quieter than hungry ones. Black storks just dump a pile of fish in the middle of the nest, and let the chicks take what they want.

What is pigeon milk?

This is a fluid rich in protein produced by cells lining the crop of male and female pigeons, used to feed the chicks. Flamingos feed their chicks in the same way: so do emperor penguins, but only the males produce the milk.

Scarlet macaws live in areas like Mexico and Bolivia.

Which birds don't look after their chicks?

Mound-building birds like the mallee fowl. They leave their eggs to hatch in a mound of sand, from which the chicks eventually scramble out. If the parents see the chicks, they do not even recognize them.

When do eggs get noisy?

Chicks of nidifugous birds make clicking sounds in the last few days before they hatch. If you play recordings of these sounds to a clutch of eggs, they will all hatch at the same time.

What is an egg-tooth?

The hardened tip of the chick's beak is called an egg-tooth. It is used to break the first hole in the eggshell just before it hatches.

Why do birds sing?

BIRDS DO NOT SING BECAUSE THEY ARE HAPPY! THE TWO MAIN reasons are to attract a mate and to defend a territory. Birds recognize the song of their own species: females are attracted to a male with a powerful and complex song, and other males are driven away from his territory.

When is preening just for show?
All birds have to preen themselves, but some species of duck go through the motions in a special way as part of their display. The bill never actually touches the feathers, but the bird raises its wing to show off the bright patch of color, that is the badge of its species.

Which bird raises a false alarm?
There can be more to alarm calls than just warning other birds of danger. In the Amazon, when several different species are feeding together, in a flock, the white-winged shrike tanager, gives an alarm call when it sees another bird find a tasty insect. All the birds fly away in fright – except the crafty tanager, which dashes in and grabs the prey.

Frigate birds have webbed feet, but are poor swimmers.

Frigate bird

Do birds have singing lessons?
Yes. In a famous experiment with chaffinches, scientists found that young males cannot develop the full song of the species without hearing adult males (or at least recordings of them) singing nearby and copying them.

Why do birds preen each other?
Mutual preening helps to remove parasites, such as ticks from places that a bird cannot reach for itself, round its head and neck. Since the only birds that do this are the two members of a breeding pair, it is usually seen as part of the "bonding" process that keeps them together.

Why do birds sing other birds' songs?
Indian hill mynas are well known for imitating human voices, though they rarely mimic other birds in the wild. But marsh warblers include quotations from hundreds of other species in their song, from both Europe and Africa. This may be because males with more complex songs win more mates. Male mocking birds in America, copy the song of another species when it approaches their territory, possibly to drive it away.

When does a frigate bird blow up?
Male frigates have a huge red throat-pouch, which they inflate to attract females, making a wavering, fluting call as they do so.

Which birds collect ring-pulls?
Male bower birds in Australia and New Guinea decorate the areas round their courtship shelters (or bowers) with brightly colored flowers, seeds and beetle wings. If the bower is near a road, they often use ring-pulls from drinks cans (thrown from car windows) in their collections.

Count Raggi's red-plumed bird of paradise uses its stunning red tail feathers to attract mates.

Count Raggi's bird of paradise

Why does one adult bird sometimes feed another?
Males often bring food to their mates, while they are incubating the eggs, presumably to save them having to go to find food for themselves. In many species this has become a ritual part of courtship. In the African hornbill it is essential, because the female uses mud to wall herself into the nest-hole until the chicks hatch. If the male didn't feed her, she would starve.

Why do birds show off?

FOR MUCH THE SAME REASONS AS THEY SING, BUT WITH MORE emphasis on finding and keeping a mate. Males may display (the technical term for showing off) and even fight while the females watch. Ruffs and capercaillie perform a mass display called a lek. Afterwards, the females choose the most successful males to breed with. The most elaborate displays are seen among birds of paradise and peacocks.

Gannet

Gannets swim under water using their feet and half-opened wings.

How do birds catch fish?

WITH THEIR BEAKS – WHICH OFTEN HAVE A HOOKED TIP OR JAGGED edges, to help them grip their prey – or with their feet, like fish eagles or ospreys. As well as long, curved talons, the feet often have roughened soles to improve the grip. The African fish eagle strikes its prey with its long hind talon and then clenches the others round it.

African fish eagle

Why do gannets end up in fishing nets?

People used to say that gannets can dive to 160 feet (50 m), because they are sometimes found caught in fishing nets set at that depth. But they stay underwater for 10 seconds or less, so they wouldn't have time to get that deep. In fact, they rarely dive more than 32 feet (10 m): the unfortunate birds in the nets must have been caught and killed as the nets were pulled up.

This African fish eagle is just about to strike its prey.

How do jays and oak trees help each other?

As WELL AS PREYING ON THE CHICKS OF OTHER BIRDS, JAYS FEED on acorns. In the fall, when acorns are plentiful, jays bury some of them to dig up later. Those that they don't find will grow into new oak trees.

Jay

Jays are very noisy birds. They have harsh, raspy voices.

Why don't woodpeckers get headaches?

When a woodpecker drills the bark of a tree, using its head as a hammer and its beak as a chisel, soft, spongy bone, between the beak and the skull, absorbs most of the impact.

When are geese like cows?

Just like cows, most species of geese feed mainly on grass Their short, sharp-edged bill is specially adapted for cutting the grass off close to the ground.

What is a bird pellet?

The indigestible remains of a bird's food, such as bones and shells, wrapped in softer left-overs like fur or wool. The bird throws up these neat packets, rather than trying to pass them through its gut.

Which bird eats only snails?

The Everglades kite, in Florida, is a genuine bird of prey, with strong talons and a sharply hooked beak, but its only food is apple snails. As the Everglades dry up, the snails are becoming scarce, which is why the kite is also becoming rare.

When is a thrush like a blacksmith?

A song thrush uses a stone, called an anvil, to kill snails, which it beats against the stone until the shell breaks.

Why are hummingbirds good for flowers?

They pollinate them when they collect nectar. Grains of pollen stick to the hummingbird's head, and are transferred to the next flower it visits.

Do birds use tools?

Yes. Woodpecker finches, in the Galapagos, use cactus spines to winkle out larvae from their burrows in dead wood, because they can't reach them with their short beaks. Egyptian vultures pick up stones and drop them on ostrich eggs to break them. Green-backed herons, in the United States, have been seen using bread as bait to bring fish within reach of their bill.

Unlike birds today, *Archaeopteryx* (shown in a fossil here) had teeth.

Fossilized
Archaeopteryx

How does a bird get waterproof feathers?

Birds preen mainly to keep their feathers clean, to get rid of dust and dirt; but there are other important reasons. Oil from the preen gland, above the bird's tail, is spread on to the feathers to keep them waterproof. This oil is changed into vitamin D by sunlight, and the bird swallows some of it when it next preens. The blades of flight feathers that have become separated can be "zipped" back together by the bird's bill.

What is molting?

Growing new feathers and casting off the old ones. As the new feathers grow, they push the old ones out of their sockets. Most birds do this once a year, though some do it twice, especially when they have different breeding and non-breeding plumages. Many migrant birds start molting before they leave the breeding grounds, stop while they are traveling, and then finish the molt, when they arrive in their wintering area. Geese molt in their breeding grounds, becoming flightless while their young grow their own flight feathers.

What is the link between feathers and dinosaurs?

Feathers are modified scales, made from a protein called beta-keratin, which is otherwise found only in lizard skin. Birds are descended from ancient lizards related to dinosaurs: the earliest known bird, *Archaeopteryx*, has many reptile-like features.

Do birds wear thermal underwear?

Down feathers are the thermal underwear of birds. They are soft and fluffy, covered by a layer of windproof feathers, trapping warm air close to the bird's skin. Chicks, like those of penguins, have very thick down, to keep them warm in the bitter cold of the Antarctic.

Do feathers grow all over a bird's body?

Feathers grow in areas called "tracts," leaving some bare skin between them – though the bare skin is often covered by down, and by feathers fanning out from the tracts. Vultures have bald heads and necks because any feathers growing there would soon be filthy with blood and fat from their food.

Do birds have whiskers?

BRISTLES ARE A SPECIAL KIND OF FEATHER, USUALLY FOUND ON the head and neck (though barn owls have them on their feet). They may protect the eyes and nostrils, or they may act as a net round the mouth of birds that catch insects in flight, like swifts and nightjars.

How many feathers does a bird have?

It varies with the species and size of the bird, with its age, and state of health, and with the season of the year. The smallest number was counted on a hummingbird, which had 940, and the largest on a mute swan, that had 25,216 feathers.

Cormorant

Cormorants are very ancient birds – their ancestors were around 40 million years ago.

Are all feathers waterproof?

No. The body feathers of water birds have curly tips that repel water, but some, like cormorants, can dive better because their wings are not completely waterproof – they don't have to carry so much air underwater. This is why they stand around with their wings hung out to dry between dives.

Why do sandgrouse lounge around in pools?

Several bird species, such as the shoebill stork, carry water to their chicks in their bills, and one species, the African sandgrouse, carries it in special feathers on its belly. Sandgrouse sit in pools until the feathers are soaked, and then fly back to their chicks.

Which birds make weird music with their feathers?

Snipe have special feathers in their tails that make a "drumming" or "bleating" sound when they dive quickly during their display flights. Mute swans make a high-pitched creaking sound with their wings as they fly.

Do birds enjoy the taste of their food?

Yes. it is important that they taste food, not only
because they can then choose to eat things with a high nutritious value, but so that they can avoid poisons, like those used by many butterflies and caterpillars in self-defence.

How does a penguin find his mate after a year at sea?
By hearing her voice. Even in densely crowded, noisy colonies, mates can recognize each other's calls, and later, those of their chicks.

Why don't cave swiftlets bump into cave walls?
They use "echolocation" to avoid obstacles in the dark. They make a buzzing sound and listen for the echoes it produces from the walls. Outside, they have a normal twittering call, but they start buzzing as soon as they enter the cave.

Is an eagle really "eagle-eyed"?
While it is true that birds of prey can see very well, of those that have been tested, only the wedge-tailed eagle can see better than humans – two and a half times better in fact. Kestrels and falcons have about the same power of sight as we do.

Do birds have an internal barometer?
Yes, they can sense small changes in air pressure. This may be important in predicting coming changes in the weather, which might tell them that it is time to migrate.

Swallow

Swallows leave cooler countries, such as northern Europe, at the end of summer, in search of warmer weather.

Woodcock

The woodcock is known for its beautiful trilling courtship songs.

Which birds can see backwards?

WOODCOCK, AND MANY DUCKS, HAVE THEIR EYES PLACED at the sides of their heads, so that they have a 360° field of vision. This enables them to watch out for approaching enemies even while they are feeding.

How does the owl turn its head back to front?

Owls have very large eyes to enable them to gather as much light as possible, and see in the dark; but this means that they cannot move their eyes in their sockets. To compensate for this, they can turn their heads through an arc of 180°.

Do ducks get cold feet?

Yes, but it doesn't harm them. A special arrangement of blood vessels cools the blood going out to the feet and warms the blood coming back, so that even when standing on ice, the duck doesn't lose too much heat.

Does a homing pigeon use a compass?

Yes. Experiments with homing pigeons, using magnets, show that they are sensitive to the earth's magnetic field, and use it to help them navigate on long journeys. Other birds probably use the same method.

Why does a kiwi have nostrils at the end of its beak?

Kiwis feed at night, in the forests of New Zealand, snuffling through the leaf litter in search of invertebrates. They find their food by scent, using the nostrils at the tip of their beak: they are the only birds to have their nostrils in this position.

How many kinds of bird are flightless?

Why is a kiwi like a bandicoot?

A bandicoot is a small insect-eating marsupial living in the forests of Australia and New Guinea. New Zealand has no native mammals, and the job of forest-floor insect-eater has been taken over by the kiwi.

THE OSTRICH FAMILY CONTAINS THE BIGGEST FLIGHTLESS BIRDS, including emus, rheas, cassowaries, and the extinct moas and elephant birds. Penguins, in the southern hemisphere, are the most numerous flightless birds, while there are only three species of kiwi, all living in New Zealand. New Zealand also has two flightless parrots, the kakapo and the kea. Other families of birds contain flightless species, such as the cormorant in the Galapagos, the steamer duck in the Falkland Islands, and rails on islands in the Indian Ocean. Also in the Indian Ocean, the dodo, and two species of solitaire, were wiped out in historical times.

A kiwi snuffles for insects on the forest floor.

Kiwi

How fast can an ostrich run?

A biologist once drove alongside a running ostrich on the Mara Plains in Kenya with his speedometer reading 36 mph (60 kph).

Ostrich

Ostriches can run faster than any other birds.

Why are some birds part-time fliers?

Because they give up flying when they molt. Geese that breed in the high Arctic can escape from the few predators that live there by swimming, so they can change all their wing feathers at once, while their goslings are growing theirs. When the time comes to fly south for the winter, the whole family has new flight feathers. Most members of the auk family also molt all their flight feathers at once.

Which bird flies underwater?

Penguins are brilliant fliers. Their narrow, sharp-edged wings are like those of a swift, and their streamlined bodies allow them to move very fast and manoeuvre with great precision. The only reason we call them "flightless" is that they do it underwater.

Which penguin is extinct?

The first bird to be called a "penguin" was the great auk, in the North Atlantic, which has been extinct for more than a hundred years. Nowadays all the true penguins live south of the Equator.

Why can few island birds fly?

Two different reasons lead to the same result. There are fewer predators on islands, so birds that usually feed on the ground don't need to be able to fly to escape; and flying is dangerous on islands, in case a wind gets up and blows the bird out to sea.

How long can a loony diver stay underwater?

The great northern diver (called the common loon in North America) is the deepest-diving bird: it has been accidentally caught on fishing lines 195 feet (60 m) underwater. Even at this great depth, it stays under for no longer than a minute: 62 seconds is the longest recorded dive.

The cassowary's hard helmet protects its head.

Cassowary

Why does a cassowary wear a helmet?

It needs one to protect its head from thorns and branches as it dashes through the forest. All that remains of its flight feathers are bare black spines, curving round its body: they too protect it, by brushing aside vines and bushes.

Why don't polar bears eat penguins?

The probably would, if they had the chance, but the only place the two might meet would be in a zoo, where the keepers are careful to keep them apart. Nature does this by having polar bears living in the Arctic, and penguins in the Antarctic.

Why is it dangerous for birds to live on islands?

U NTIL HUMANS CAME ALONG, ISLANDS WERE AMONG THE safest places for birds to live, but people soon changed that. The first danger came from passing sailors, who came ashore for water and wood, and without knowing it, brought rats with them. Rats are very good predators on island birds. When people started to live in the islands, cats and dogs, and even pigs, continued the damage started by the rats.

How many of the world's bird species are endangered?
Eleven per cent, most of them because of the harm done by people to the natural environment. Draining wetlands and felling forests are the main causes of damage, but the misuse of pesticides and industrial pollution also play a part.

Where is the endangered barn owl a pest?
In the Seychelles, where someone had the bright idea of introducing barn owls from South Africa to kill rats. They instantly started killing birds instead, especially fairy terns, and taking over the nest-sites of the rare Seychelles kestrel.

Dodos were land birds with thick, heavy feathers.

Dodo

Who ate the dodo and the solitaire?
The dodo was a large, flightless pigeon living on Mauritius. All dodos were wiped out when people first came to their islands. Some were eaten by people, and the rest by introduced pigs and rats. By the middle of the 18th century they were all extinct.

Why does the Californian condor owe its survival to a glove puppet?

When condors, nearly extinct in the wild, were being bred in captivity, scientists wanted to avoid the chicks becoming too familiar with humans. They fed them with meat held in a glove puppet, that looked like a condor's head.

Why is the néné important?

The néné was the first bird species to be bred in captivity – at the Wildfowl and Wetlands Trust in England and in Hawaii – with the intention of releasing it back into its home, when it was safe to do so. The operation was a success.

Néné

The néné, also called the Hawaiin goose, has been saved from extinction by being bred in captivity.

Why was North America's commonest bird made extinct?

Before 1840 there were thousands of millions of passenger pigeons in North America, but they were slaughtered for food until only one was left – a female called Martha – who died at 12 years old in 1914, in a zoo in Ohio.

What is Ducks Unlimited?

An organization of North American duck-hunters. They check the breeding success of wild ducks each year, to work out how many they can shoot for food and for sport without endangering the population.

Who is destroying the world's forests?

The increasing human population. In the tropics, people clear forests to grow food for their families or for large companies. The demand for large timber in Europe, North America, and Japan is all too often met by chopping down irreplaceable ancient forests.

How many kinds of bird have become extinct?

MORE THAN 150 SINCE 1600 – THAT WE KNOW ABOUT – AND probably many more, that no one ever noticed. It wasn't just European explorers who did the damage: archaeology shows that when people first arrived in ancient times on Hawaii, and islands in the South Pacific and the Caribbean, they killed many birds that Europeans never even saw.

Why do birds throw away their eggshells?

BECAUSE THE WHITE INSIDE OF THE SHELL WOULD

attract predators. Most ground-nesting birds carry their eggshells quite a distance from the nest, before dropping them. This was proved in a famous experiment, with gulls, by the great ornithologist Niko Tinbergen.

Peregrine falcon

The peregrine falcon is a fast, strong flier and hunts from several hundred feet in the air.

Which bird escaped to Malta

In the reign of Henri IV, of France (1553–1610), a peregrine falcon with a gold band bearing its master's name escaped. It was found 24 hours later in Malta, 1,300 miles (2,160 km) away. It was common at the time to mark hunting birds, and also some quarry birds, such as herons with rings.

How do amateur enthusiasts study bird migration?

All over the world, groups of amateurs, as well as full-time scientists, trap birds to fit numbered lightweight metal rings to their legs and release them. Some of the birds are found again, dead or alive, often in countries far away. Ringing birds in this way is called "banding."

What is a mist-net?

A fine net, supported on poles, used to trap birds for banding. The strands are too thin for the birds to see in time to avoid being caught.

What is a sonogram?

This is a means of printing out the sounds birds make so that they can be studied. A sonogram shows the frequency of the sound and the time it lasts.

What are Darwin's finches?

A group of related finch species living in the Galapagos. They differ from island to island. When Charles Darwin visited the islands in 1835, he studied the differences between the finches. His findings led to his discovery of the theory of evolution.

What is a duck decoy?

An old way of catching ducks for food, that is sometimes still used today by bird-ringers. The ducks follow a dog into a tapering tunnel of netting, called a pipe, until the tunnel is too narrow for them to escape. They follow the dog as they would a fox, probably to watch it, in case it is hunting them.

How do you count birds?

THERE ARE MANY WAYS, SOME INVOLVING BANDING AND recapturing birds, and some done just by watching. The most reliable way to study bird populations is during the breeding season, when the adults are busy at their nests.

One of the best places to count birds is from a beach. This is called a "sea watch."

Birdwatching

What is a honey guide?

Honeyguide

A SMALL AFRICAN BIRD THAT FEEDS ON BEE larvae, honey, and beeswax from wild bees' nests. It has learned to show humans as well as ratels (or honey-badgers) where bees' nests are, by fluttering around them and calling until they follow it. When the ratel (or the human) breaks open the nest to get the honey, the honey-guide has a free feed.

The honeyguide watches the honey badger, waiting for its honey feast.

Why do cattle egrets follow buffalo?
To help them find their food. Cattle egrets are small white herons. They feed on insects, and other small animals that are disturbed by large animals moving through grass.

What is falconry?
The ancient sport of using trained falcon (birds of prey) to hunt. Particularly in some Arab countries, the catch is still taken for human food, though in other places the main point of falconry is to watch the chase.

Why do gulls follow the plough?
Gulls do this because they have learnt that, as the plough turns over the soil, it exposes lots of good things to eat.

When did bluetits learn to open milk bottles?
This habit was first noticed in 1929, in England, when milk began to be delivered in bottles with foil tops. No one can imagine how the first bluetit discovered how to get at the creamy milk, but before long they were doing it all over the country.

Why do rhinos like ox-peckers to perch on them?
Ox-peckers, or tick-birds, are members of the starling family that feed only on the skin parasites of large mammals. They have very sharp beaks and claws, and stiff tails like a woodpecker's to support them as they perch on the animal's body. All large mammals put up with their scratchy feet – and their habit of pulling out hair to line their nests – because they remove troublesome parasites.

Why might GM foods harm wild birds?
Some genetically modified crops are designed to survive being sprayed with weedkiller. If these plants are widely used, more weedkiller will be used, until there are no weeds round the edges of fields. Many small birds, such as goldfinches, feed on weed seeds like thistles.

28

Which bird acts as a crocodile's toothbrush?
This alarming task is undertaken by spur-winged plovers, which perch on the crocodile's open jaws as it lies with its mouth open to cool off on the bank of a stream. They remove scraps of meat and probably also parasites from the crocodile's gums.

Caption

How can a bird bring down a jet plane?

Why would a dabchick follow a flamingo?
Because the foot-movements that flamingos use to stir up the mud, before they filter it for food, also disturb small animals for the dabchick to eat.

THE GREATEST DANGER IS THAT A LARGE BIRD, OR A FLOCK OF small ones, like starlings, might be sucked into the air intake of the engine, causing it to stop. But sometimes a bird crashes through the cockpit windscreen and injures the pilot.

Which is the wisest bird?

THE EGYPTIAN GOD OF WISDOM WAS OFTEN

drawn with the head of a sacred ibis, while in ancient Greece the little owl was dedicated to Athene, the goddess of wisdom. To this day, the scientific name for the little owl is Athene.

Thoth

Can birds predict thunder?

Farmers say that if the dawn chorus is late there will be a storm. This makes sense. The dawn chorus starts at first light, and if heavy clouds make the morning dark, birds will start to sing late, or not at all.

Can we forecast the weather from feeding swifts?

Swifts catch insects on the wing, so when the insects are flying high, so do the swifts. Insects fly higher in windier weather, when rain is more likely: so high-feeding swifts may be a sign of rain. On the other hand, insects fly low in humid or thundery weather. Take your pick!

Why is a bald eagle called "bald"?

Because it is piebald, or black and white – not because it doesn't have any hair (or feathers)!

What is a thunderbird?

It depends where you are in the world. In ancient Zimbabwe, lightning birds were said to look rather like eagles – they were put up to keep storms away. In North America the Indians call the tiny ruby-throated hummingbird a thunderbird, because it makes miniature thunder noises with its wings as it flies. The Romans thought a woodpecker drumming on the sacred oak (the "thunder tree") would bring rain, and this belief survived in Britain after the Romans had left.

The Egyptian god of wisdom, Thoth, had the head of a bird and the body of a man

Lightning bird

This lightning bird is carved from soapstone.

Why do people say that a tumbling rook brings rain?
It doesn't, but the weather in Britain is so hard to predict that people will try anything! Rooks perform their tumbling display flights in the fall, and it often rains in the fall, so the flights are often followed by rain.

When is an eel really a bird?

WHEN IT'S AN AVOCET. ONE OLD COUNTRY NAME FOR THE

avocet was "awl," like a cobbler's tool, because of its sharp, curved bill. The old English word for this, was pronounced more like "eel." Some birds have more than one name, depending on what people notice most about them. The lapwing, named for the way it flies, is also called "peewit" after its call, and "green plover" because that is what it looks like. In Portugal, where they migrate in winter, lapwings are called "birds of winter."

"Seagull, seagull, sit on the sand; it's never good weather when you're on the land." Or so they say, and there is some truth in it. When the wind blows hard towards the land, gulls often come ashore to feed: and that is the worst weather for fishermen.

Why doesn't one swallow make a summer in the UK?
Because although the first swallows usually arrive at the end of March and in early April, they come only in ones and twos: the main migration arrives at the end of April, when summer is really on its way. This saying is not really about birds at all: it means "one piece of good luck doesn't mean that everything will be OK from now on."

Avocet

The avocet sweeps its curved bill backwards and forwards in the water in search of food.

Index

ABC

DEF

GHIJ

KL

MNO

PQR

STU

VWXYZ